POPULAR SONGS

· F · O · R ·

HARMONICA

ARRANGED BY ERIC J. PLAHNA

D0503916

ISBN 978-1-5400-1210-4

HAL•LEONARD®

Visit Hal Leonard Online at
www.halleonard.com

Contact Us:
Hal Leonard
7777 West Bluemound Road
Milwaukee, WI 53213
Email: info@halleonard.com

In Europe contact:
Hal Leonard Europe Limited
42 Wigmore Street
Marylebone, London, W1U 2RN
Email: info@halleonardeurope.com

In Australia contact:
Hal Leonard Australia Pty. Ltd.
4 Lentara Court
Cheltenham, Victoria, 3192 Australia
Email: info@halleonard.com.au

CONTENTS

HARMONICA NOTATION LEGEND

Harmonica music can be notated two different ways: on a *musical staff*, and in *tablature*.

THE MUSICAL STAFF shows pitches and rhythms and is divided by bar lines into measures. Pitches are named after the first seven letters of the alphabet.

TABLATURE graphically represents the harmonica music. Each note will be accompanied by a number, 1 through 10, indicating what hole you are to play. The arrow that follows indicates whether to blow or draw. (All examples are shown using a C diatonic harmonica.)

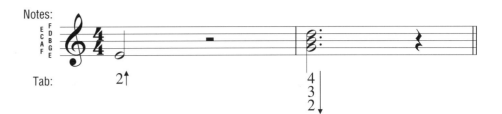

Blow (exhale) into 2nd hole.

Draw (inhale) 2nd, 3rd, & 4th holes together.

Notes on the C Harmonica

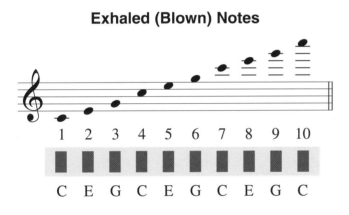

Exhaled (Blown) Notes

Inhaled (Drawn) Notes

Bends

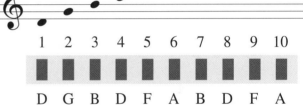

Blow Bends		Draw Bends	
	• 1/4 step		• 1/4 step
	• 1/2 step		• 1/2 step
	• 1 step		• 1 step
	• 1 1/2 steps		• 1 1/2 steps

Bad, Bad Leroy Brown

Words and Music by Jim Croce

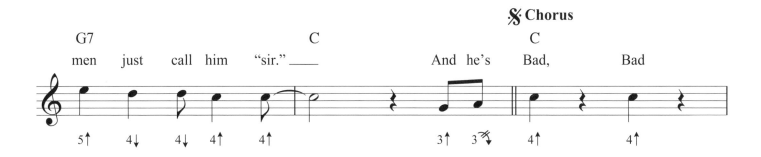

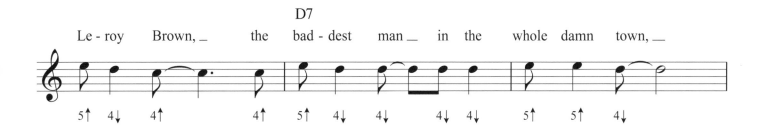

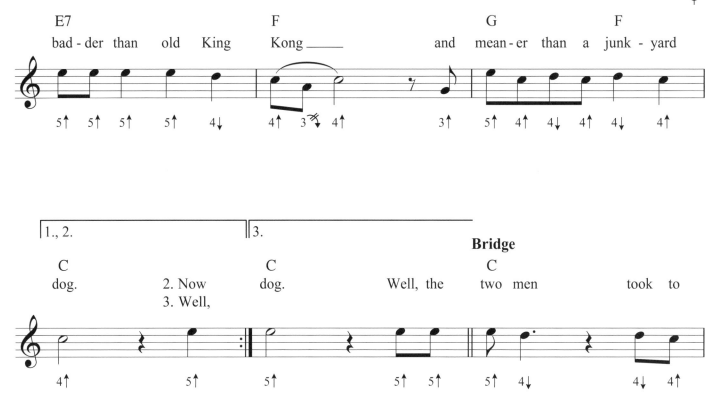

Additional Lyrics

2. Now Leroy, he a gambler and he like his fancy clothes.
And he like to wave his diamond rings in front of ev'rybody's nose.
He got a custom Continental; he got a Eldorado, too.
He got a thirty-two gun in his pocket for fun; he's got a razor in his shoe.

3. Well, Friday 'bout a week ago, Leroy shootin' dice.
And at the edge of the bar sat a girl name of Doris, and oh, that girl looked nice.
Well, he cast his eyes upon her, and the trouble soon began.
And Leroy Brown, he learned a lesson 'bout a-messin' with the wife of a jealous man.

Do You Believe in Magic

Words and Music by John Sebastian

Verse

Outro

Can't Smile Without You

Words and Music by Chris Arnold, David Martin and Geoff Morrow

*Music sounds one octave higher than written.

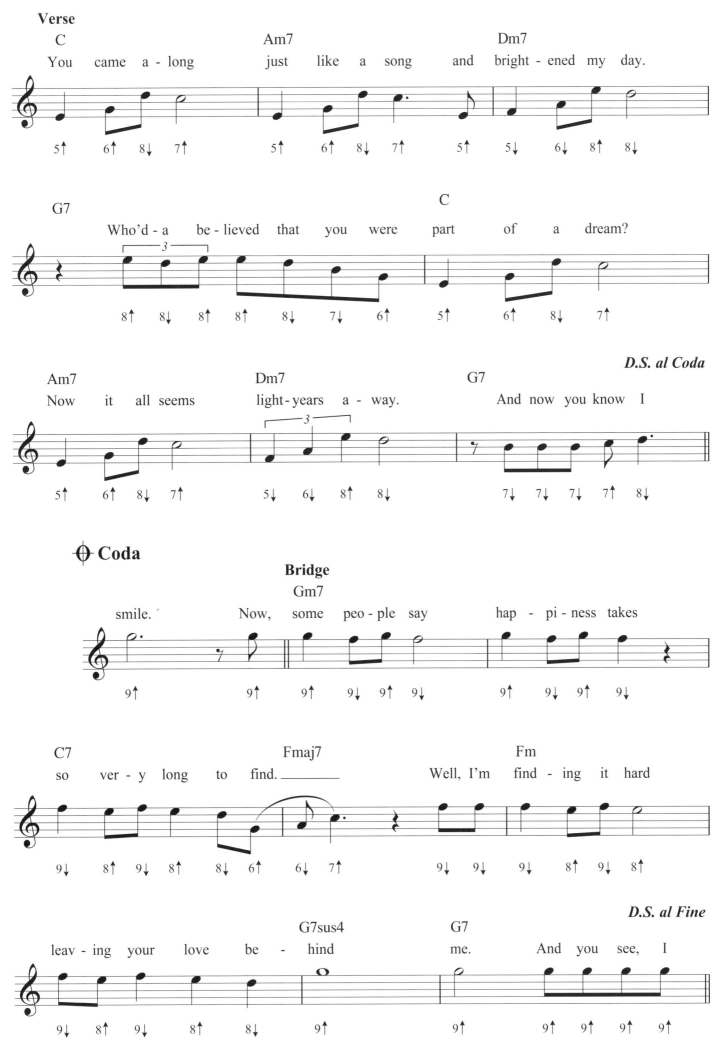

Carry On Wayward Son

Words and Music by Kerry Livgren

Despacito

**Words and Music by Luis Fonsi, Erika Ender, Justin Bieber,
Jason Boyd, Marty James Garton and Ramon Ayala**

*Music sounds one octave higher than written.

20

Additional Lyrics

5. Ya, ya me está gustando más de lo normal.
   Todos mis sentidos van pidiendo más.
   Esto hay que tomarlo sin ningún apuro.

7., 13. Dejáme sobrepasar tus zonas de peligro.
   Hasta provocar tus gritos,
   Y que olvides tu apellido.

9. Ven prueba de mi boca para ver como te sabe.
   Quiero, quiero, quiero ver cuánto amor a ti te cabe.
   Yo no tengo prisa, yo me quiero dar el viaje,
   Empecemos lento, despúes salvaje.

10. Pasito a pasito, suave savecito.
   Nos vamos pegando poquito a poquito
   Cuando tú me besas con esa destreza,
   Veo que eres malicia con delicadeza.

11. Pasito a pasito, sauve suavecito.
   No vamos pegando poquito a poquito.
   Y es que esa belleza en un rompecabezas,
   Pero pa' montarlo aquí tengo la pieza. ¡O ye!

Don't Know Why

Words and Music by Jesse Harris

Downtown

Words and Music by Tony Hatch

Pre-Chorus

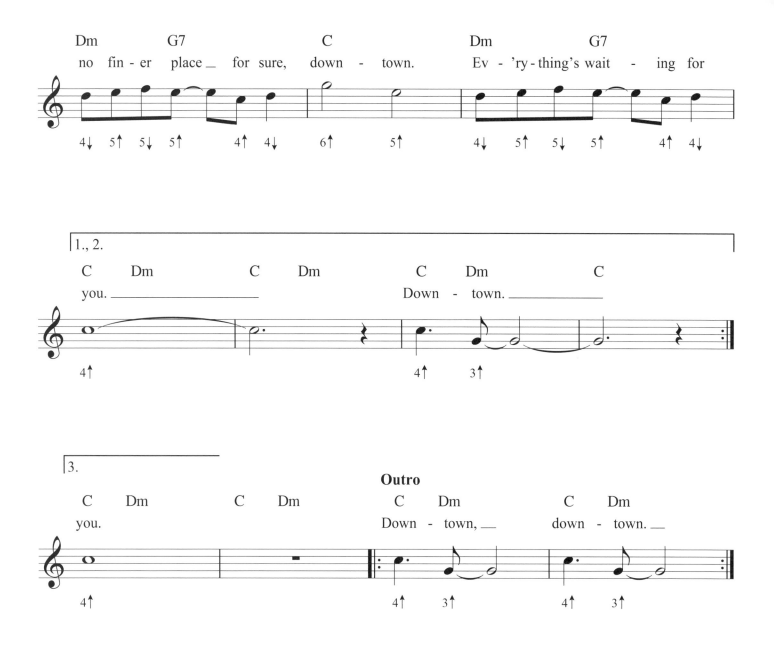

Additional Lyrics

Pre-Chorus 2. Just listen to the rhythm of the gentle bossa nova.
You'll be dancing with them too, before the night is over;
Happy again. The lights are much brighter there,
You can forget all your troubles, forget all your cares.

3. And you may find somebody kind to help and understand you.
Someone who is just like you and need a gentle hand to
Guide them along. So, maybe I'll see you there,
We can forget all our troubles, forget all our cares.

Chorus 2. So, go downtown, where all the lights are bright.
Downtown, waiting for you tonight,
Downtown, you're gonna be alright now.

3. So, go downtown, things'll be great when you're
Downtown, don't wait a minute more,
Downtown, ev'rything's waiting for you.

Good Riddance
(Time of Your Life)

Words by Billie Joe
Music by Green Day

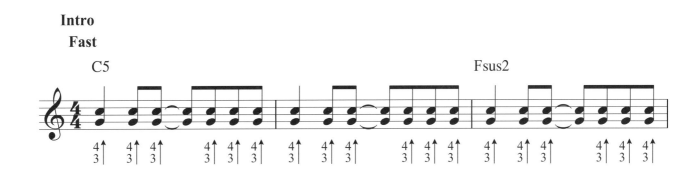

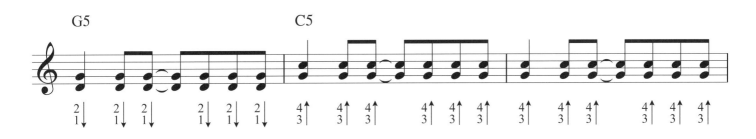

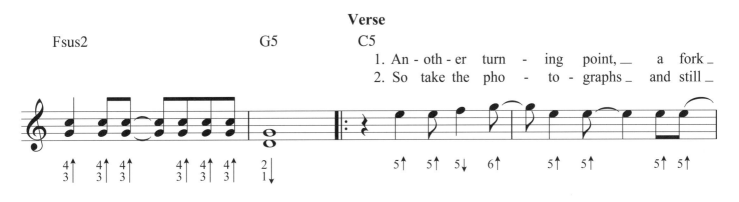

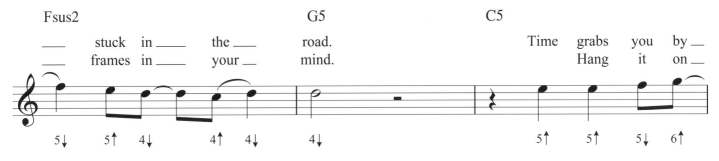

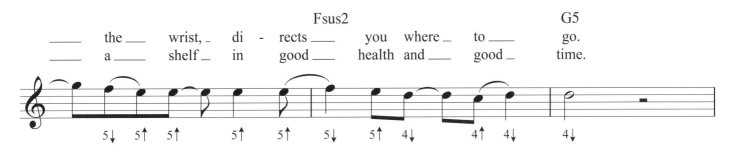

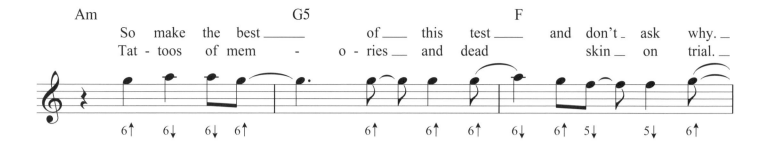

Am   **G5**   **F**

So make the best _____ of __ this test __ and don't ask why. __
Tat - toos of mem - o - ries __ and dead skin __ on trial. __

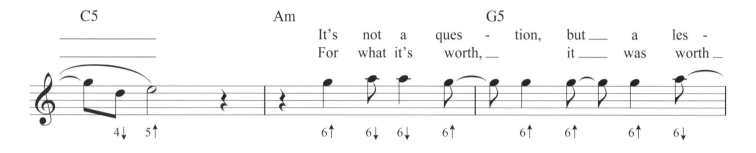

C5   **Am**   **G5**

_____ It's not a ques - tion, but __ a les -
_____ For what it's worth, __ it ___ was worth __

𝄋 Chorus

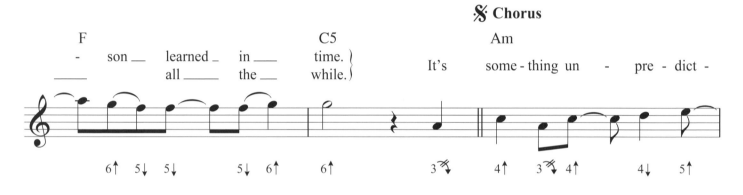

F   **C5**   **Am**

- son __ learned _ in __ time. ⎫
_____ all ___ the __ while. ⎭   It's some - thing un - pre - dict -

C5   **Am**   **C5**

- a - ble, __ but in the end __ is right. __   I

Interlude

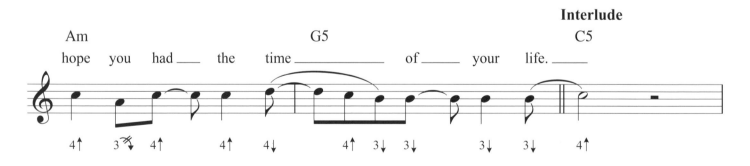

Am   **G5**   **C5**

hope you had __ the time _____ of _____ your life. _____

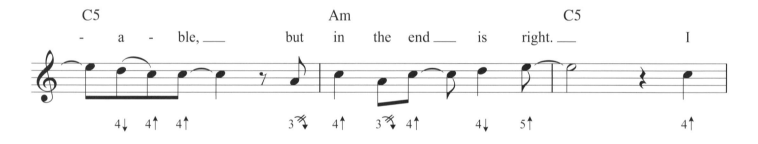

                     Fsus2   **G5**   **C5**

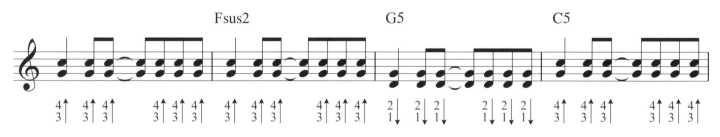

Drops of Jupiter (Tell Me)

Words and Music by Pat Monahan, James Stafford,
Robert Hotchkiss, Charles Colin and Scott Underwood

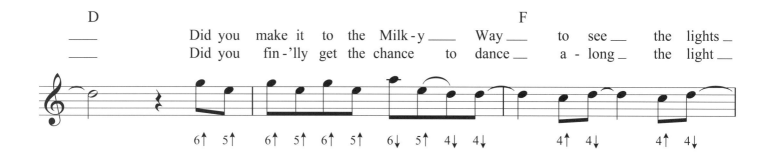

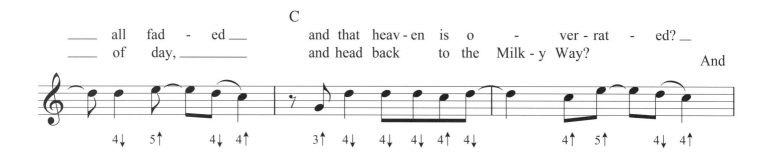

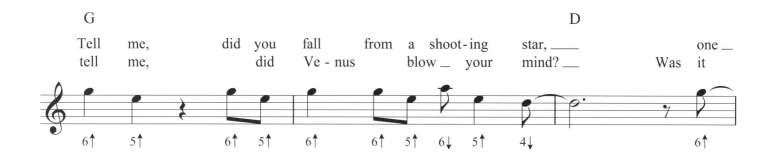

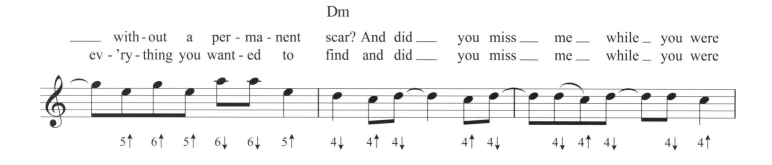

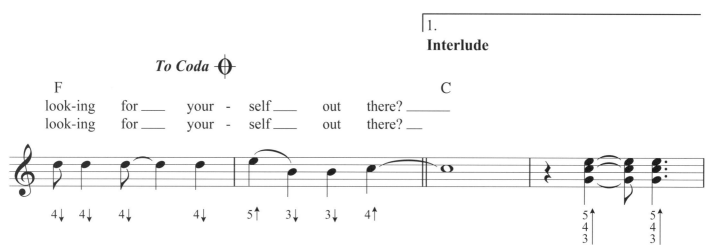

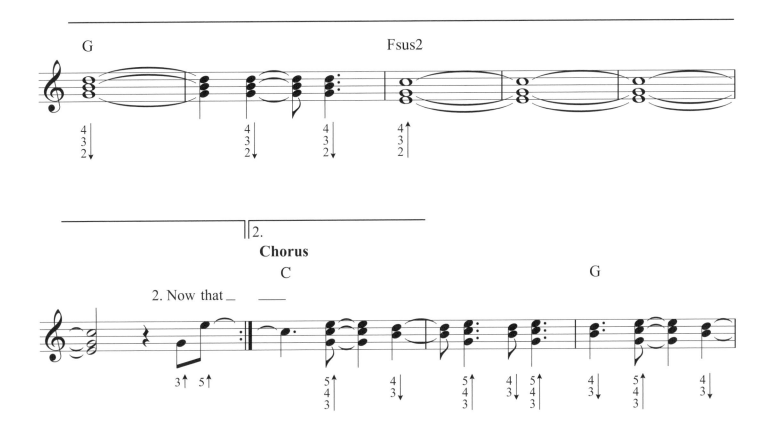

Chorus

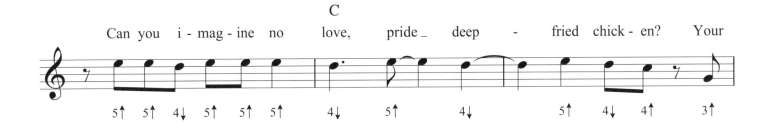

Can you i - mag - ine no love, pride _ deep - fried chick - en? Your

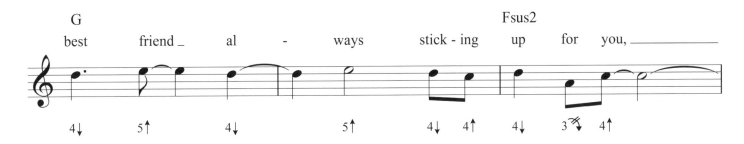

best friend _ al - ways stick - ing up for you, _____

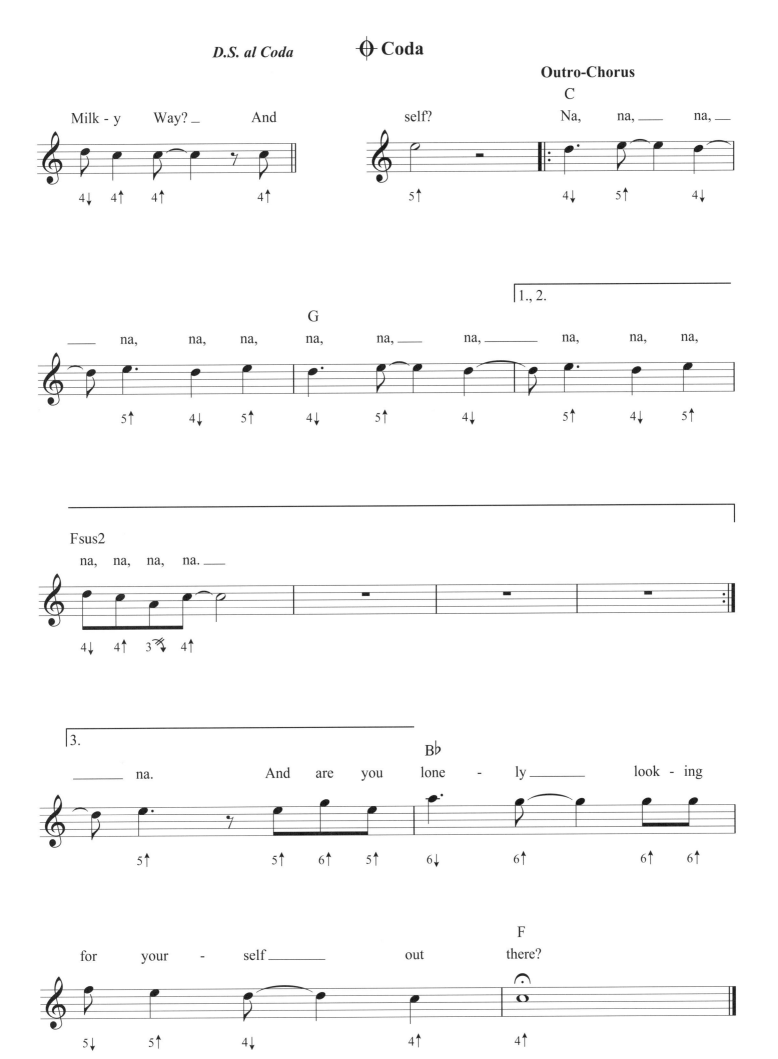

Eye of the Tiger

Theme from ROCKY III
Words and Music by Frank Sullivan and Jim Peterik

Intro

Moderate Rock

Verse

1. Ris- in' up, _____ back on the street, _____ did my time, _ took my chanc - es. Went the dis - tance, now I'm back on my feet, just a man _____ and his will to sur - vive. _

Verse

2. So man - y times _ it
3., 4. *See additional lyrics*

hap - pens too fast, _____ you trade your pas - sion for glo - ry.

*Music sounds one octave higher than written.

Additional Lyrics

3. Face to face, out in the heat,
   Hangin' tough, stayin' hungry.
   They stack the odds, still we take to the street
   For the kill with the skill to survive.

4. Risin' up, straight to the top.
   Had the guts, got the glory.
   Went the distance, now I'm not gonna stop.
   Just a man and his will to survive.

Firework

**Words and Music by Katy Perry, Mikkel Eriksen,
Tor Erik Hermansen, Esther Dean and Sandy Wilhelm**

*Music sounds one octave higher than written.

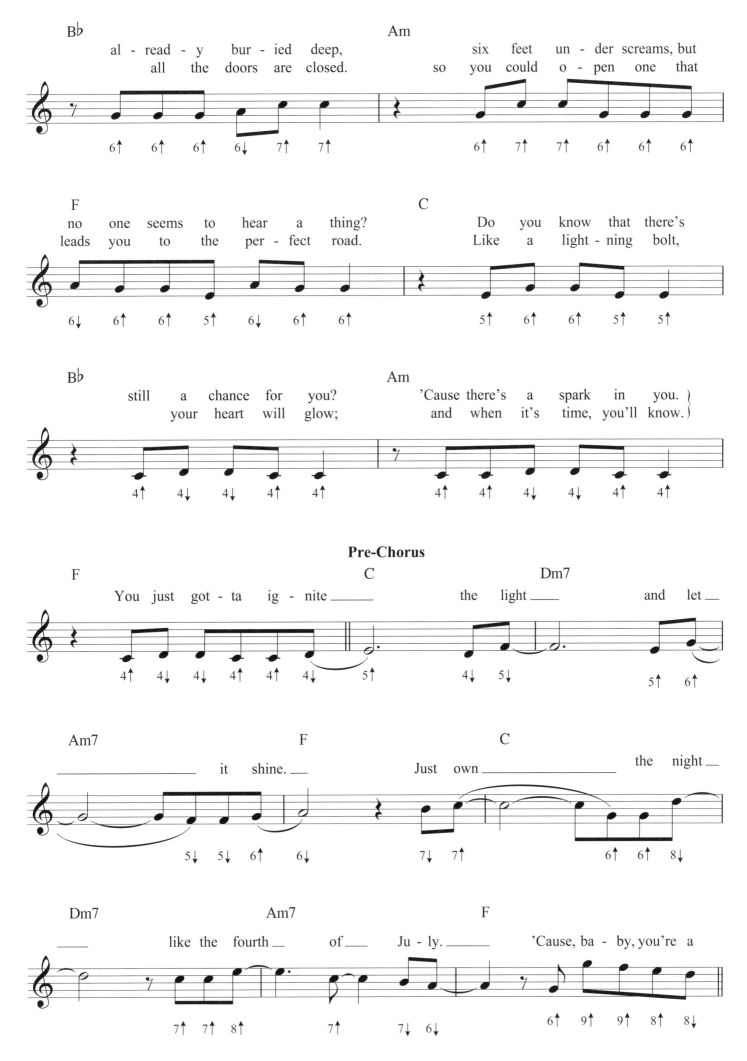

41

Fly Like an Eagle

Words and Music by Steve Miller

*Music sounds one octave higher than written.

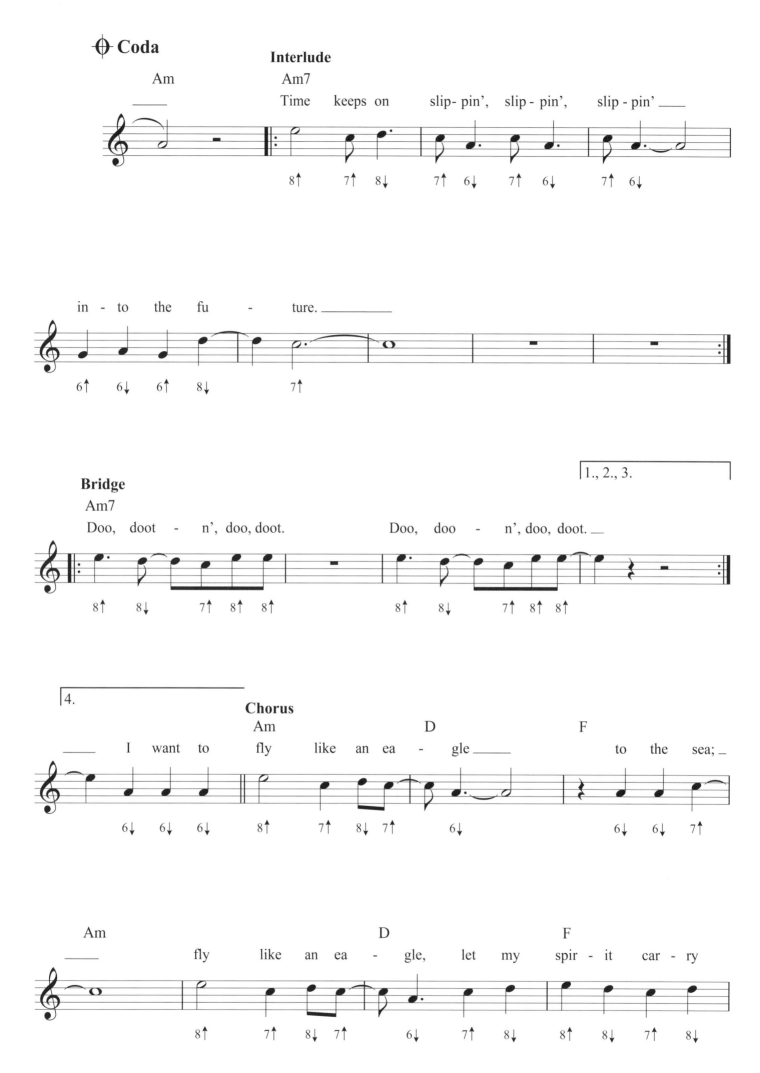

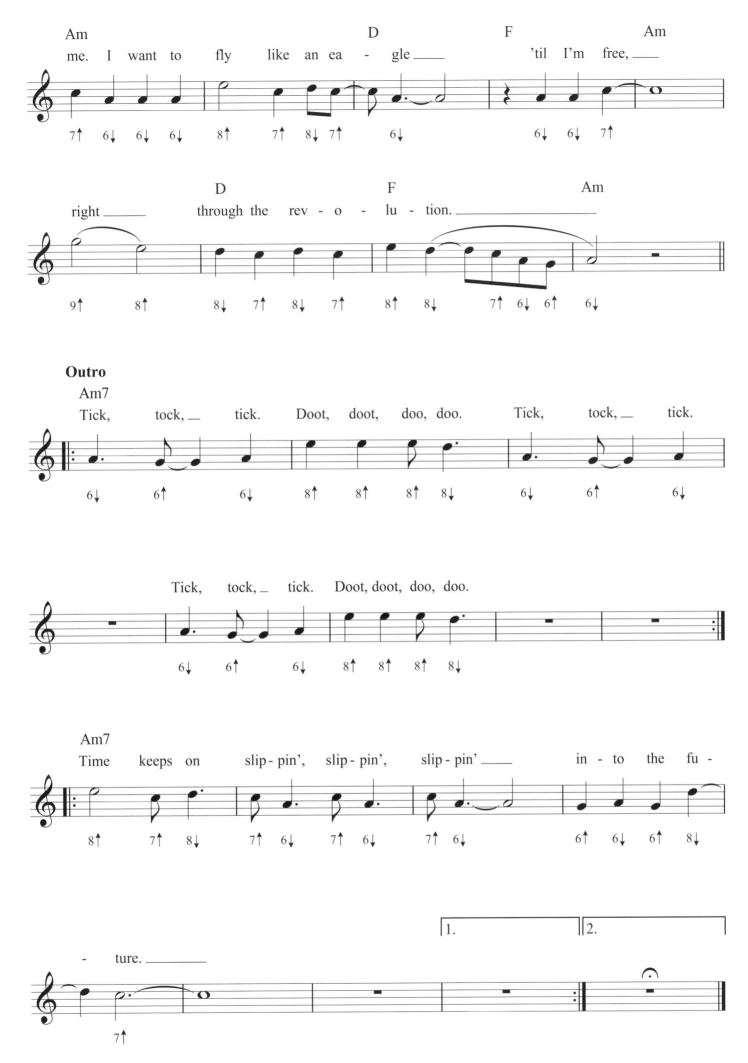

Hello

Words and Music by Adele Adkins and Greg Kurstin

*Music sounds one octave higher than written.

Am	C		G	F
Cal - i - for - nia dream - ing a - bout who we used __ to be when we were				
typ - i - cal __ of me to talk __ a - bout my - self __ I'm sor - ry I				

5↑ 5↑ 5↑   5↑ 5↑ 4↓ 4↓   4↑   4↓ 5↑ 4↓   3↗ 4↑ 4↑ 4↑ 5↑

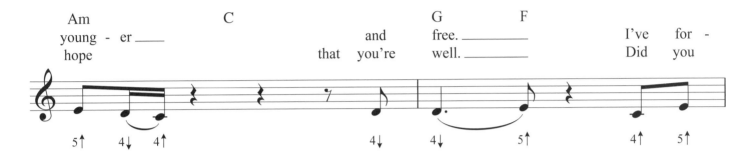

Am	C		G	F
young - er ____ and free. _____ I've for -				
hope that you're well. _____ Did you				

5↑ 4↓ 4↑   4↓   4↓ 5↑   4↑ 5↑

Am	C		G	F
got - ten how __ it felt be - fore __ the world fell at __ our feet. There's such a				
ev - er make __ it out of that town where noth - ing ev - - er hap - pened? It's no				

5↑ 5↑ 5↑   5↑ 5↑ 4↓ 4↓   4↑   4↓ 5↑ 4↓   3↗ 4↑ 4↑ 4↑ 5↑

Pre-Chorus

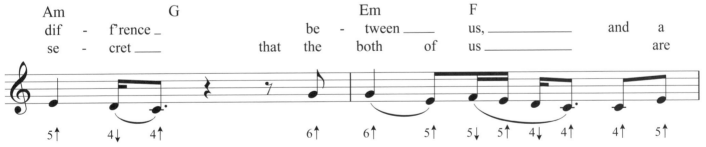

Am	G		Em	F
dif - f'rence __ be - tween ____ us, _____ and a				
se - cret ____ that the both of us _____ are				

5↑ 4↓ 4↑   6↑ 6↑ 5↑ 5↓ 5↑ 4↓ 4↑ 4↑ 5↑

𝄋 **Chorus**

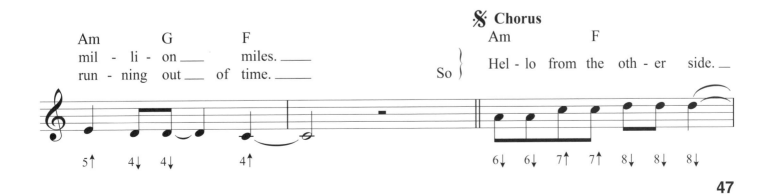

Am	G	F		Am	F
mil - li - on ___ miles. ___			So {	Hel - lo from the oth - er side. ___	
run - ning out __ of time. ___					

5↑ 4↓ 4↓   4↑   6↓ 6↓ 7↑ 7↑ 8↓ 8↓ 8↓

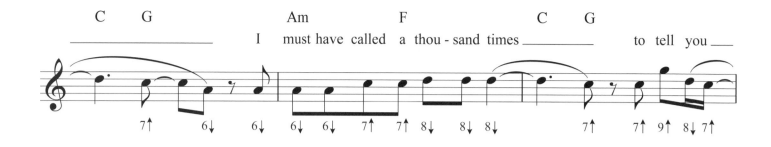

I must have called a thou-sand times to tell you

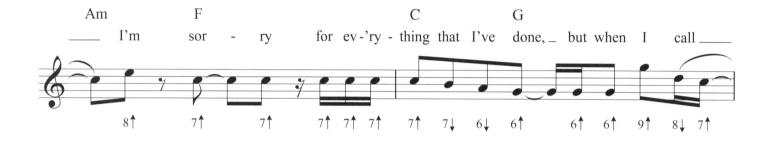

I'm sor - ry for ev-'ry-thing that I've done, but when I call

you nev - er seem to be home. Hel - lo from the out - side.

At least I can say that I've tried to tell you

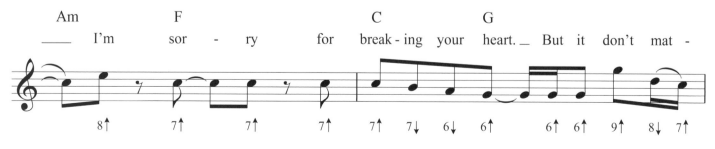

I'm sor - ry for break-ing your heart. But it don't mat -

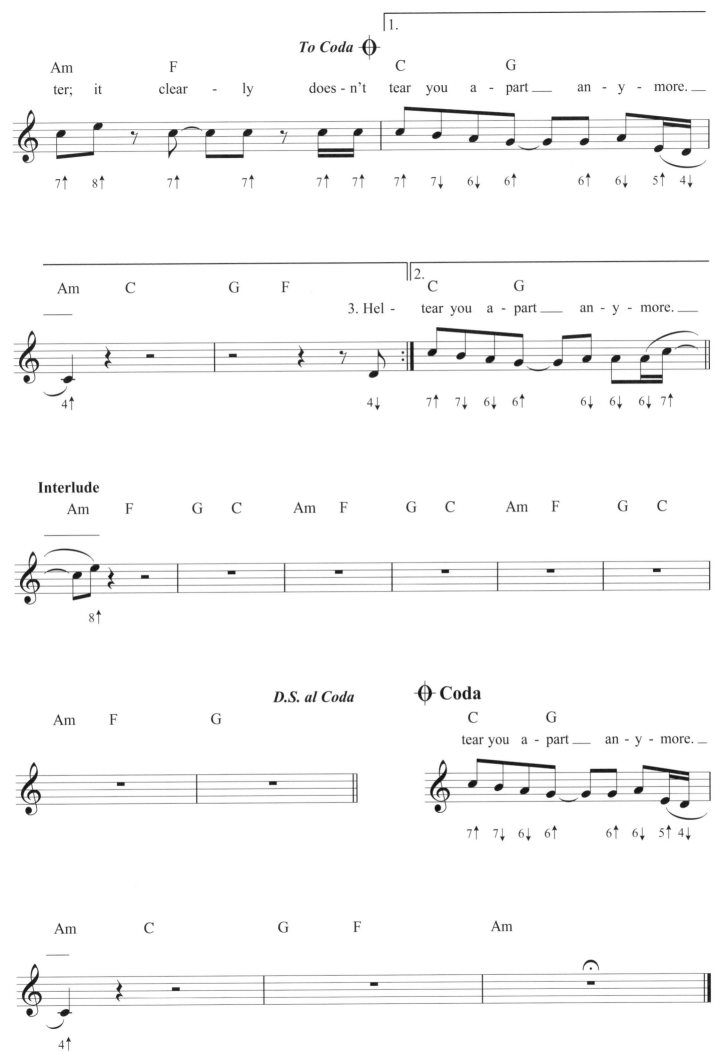

Home

Words and Music by Greg Holden and Drew Pearson

The trou-ble,___ it might drag___ you

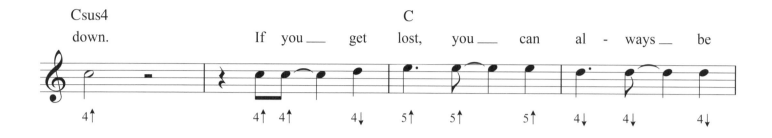

down. If you___ get lost, you___ can al - ways___ be

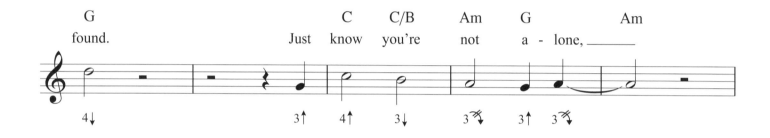

found. Just know you're not a - lone,_____

'cause I'm gon - na make this place your_____

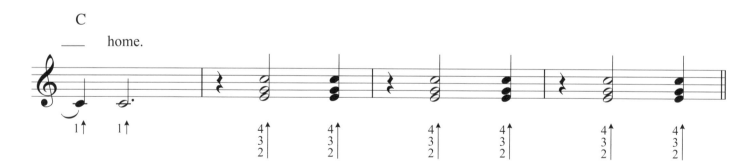

___ home.

Chorus

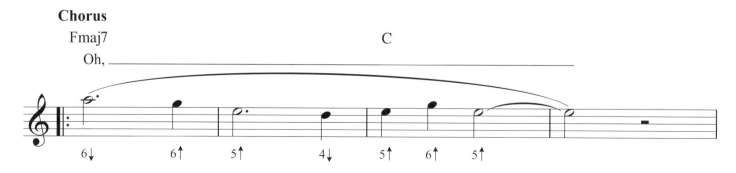

Oh,_____

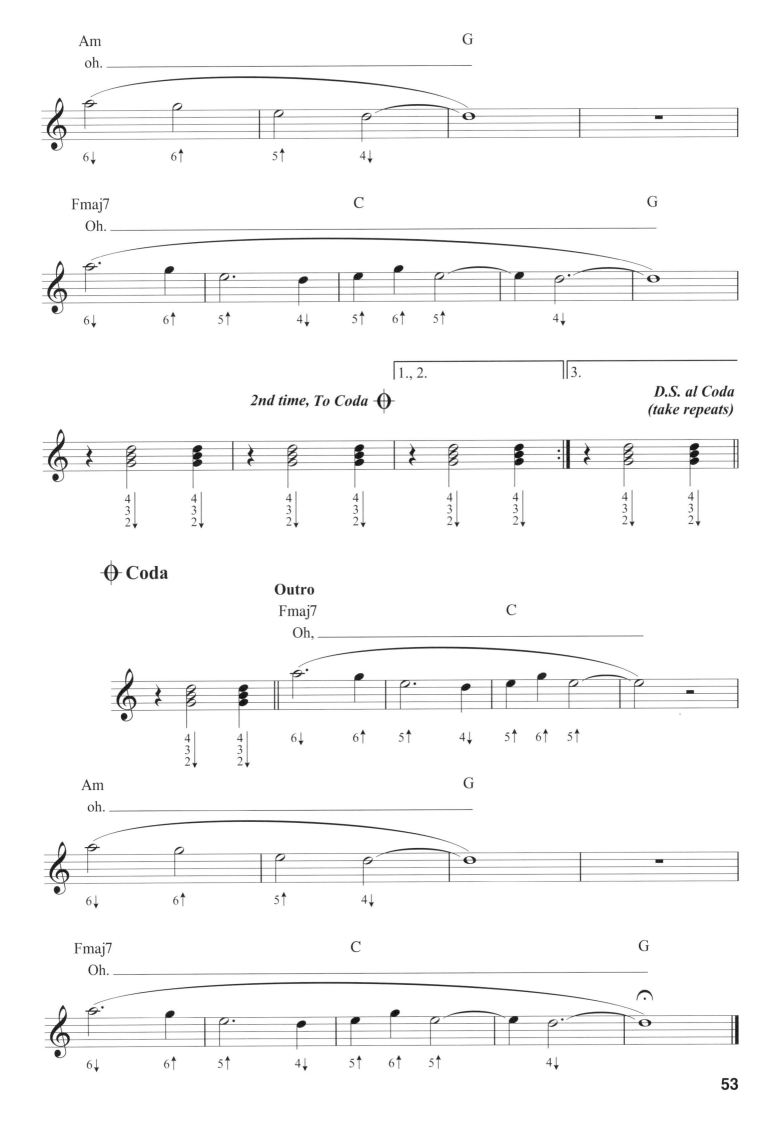

I'd Like to Teach the World to Sing

Words and Music by Bill Backer, Roquel Davis, Roger Cook and Roger Greenaway

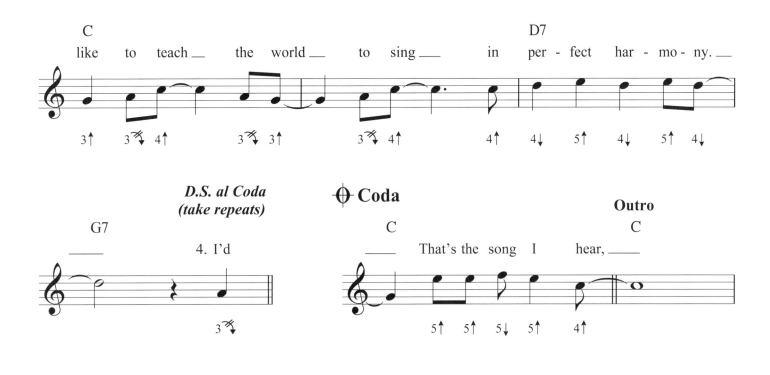

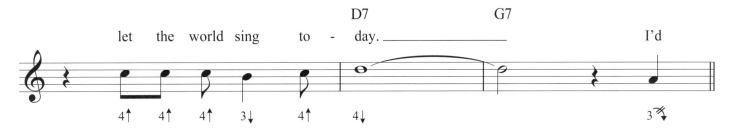

Additional Lyrics

2., 5. I'd like to teach the world to sing in perfect harmony,
I'd like to hold it in my arms and keep it company.

3., 6. I'd like to see the world for once all standing hand in hand,
And hear them echo through the hills for peace throughout the land.

Ironic

Lyrics by Alanis Morissette
Music by Alanis Morissette and Glen Ballard

Bridge

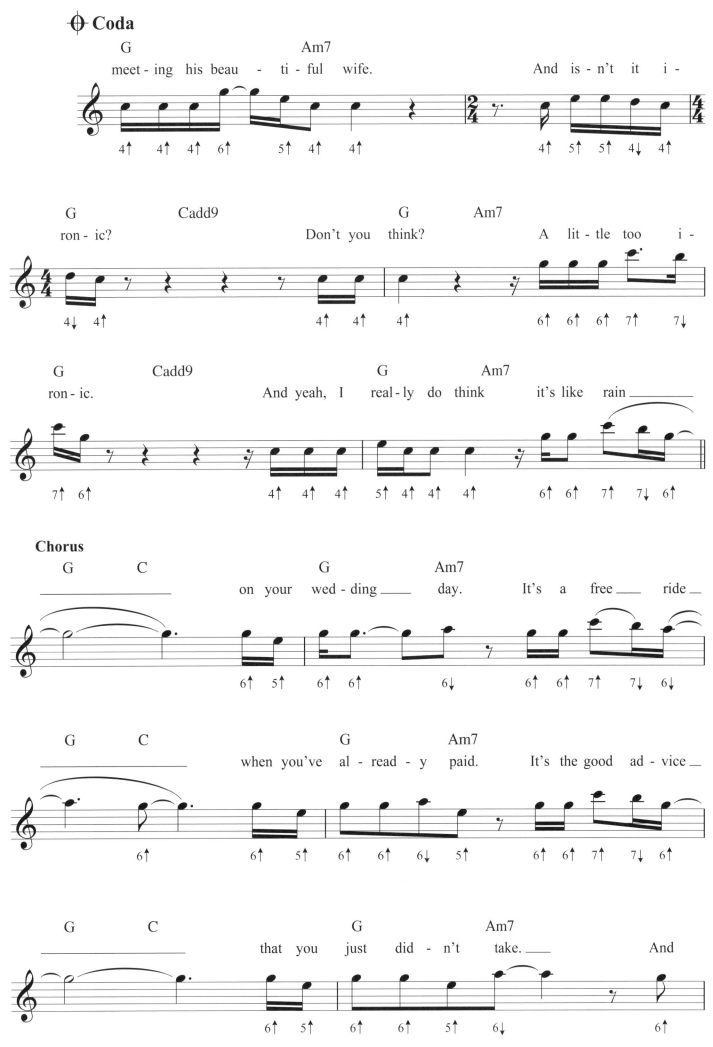

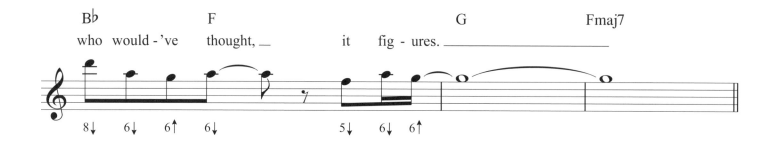

Outro

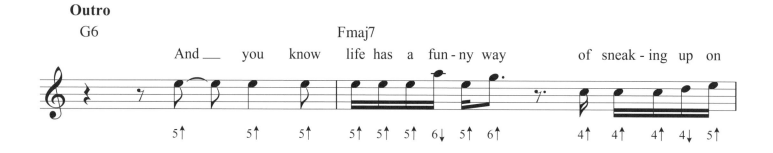

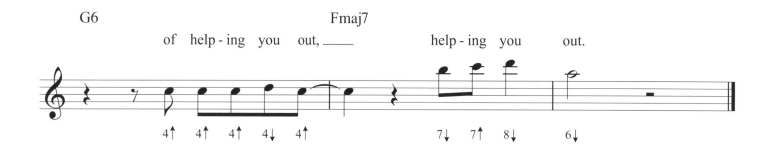

Additional Lyrics

2. Mister Play-It-Safe was too afraid to fly.
   He packed his suitcase and kissed his kids goodbye.
   He waited his whole damn life to take that flight,
   And as the plane crashed down, he thought, "Well, isn't this nice..."

3. A traffic jam when you're already late.
   A "No Smoking" sign on your cigarette break.
   It's like ten tousand spoons when all you need is a knife.
   It's meeting the man of my dreams, and then meeting his beautiful wife.

No Matter What

Written by Peter Ham

*Music sounds one octave higher than written.

Losing My Religion

Words and Music by William Berry, Peter Buck, Michael Mills and Michael Stipe

Intro
Moderately

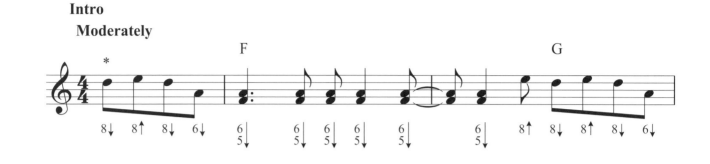

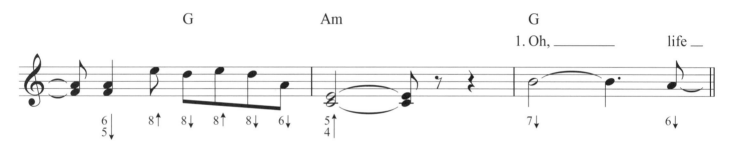

Verse

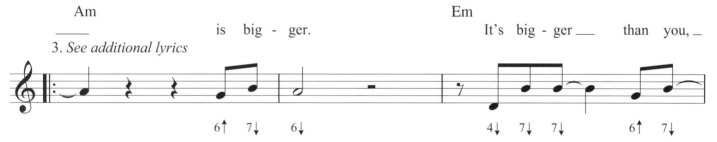

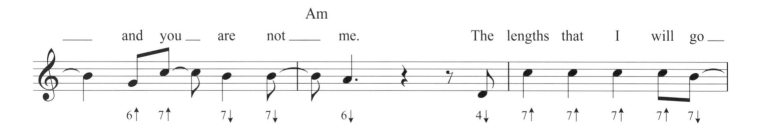

*Music sounds one octave higher than written.

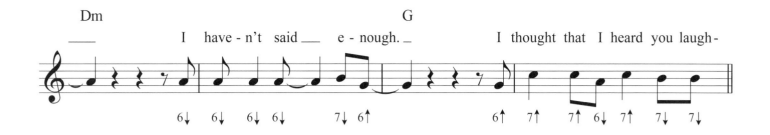

Chorus

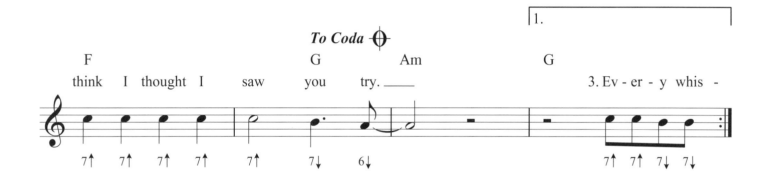

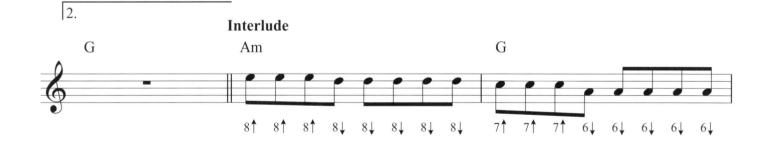

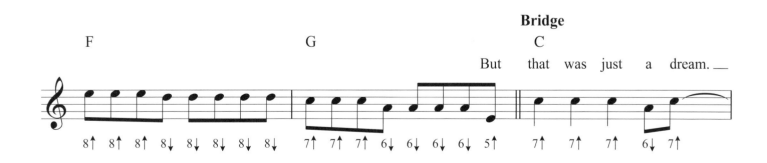

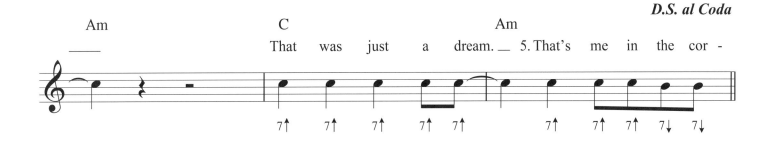

⊕ Coda

Outro

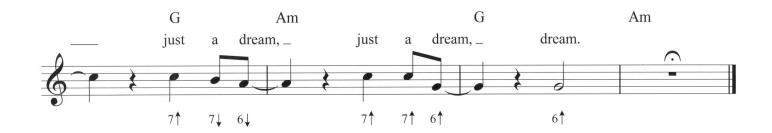

Additional Lyrics

3. Every whisper of ev'ry waking hour,
   I'm choosing my confessions,
   Trying to keep an eye on you like a hurt, lost and blind fool, fool.
   Oh no, I've said too much. I set it up.

4. Consider this, consider this the hint of the century.
   Consider this: the slip that brought me to my knees failed.
   What if all these fantasies come flailing around?
   And now, I've said too much.

Mack the Knife

from THE THREEPENNY OPERA

English Words by Marc Blitzstein
Original German Words by Bert Brecht
Music by Kurt Weill

*Music sounds one octave higher than written.

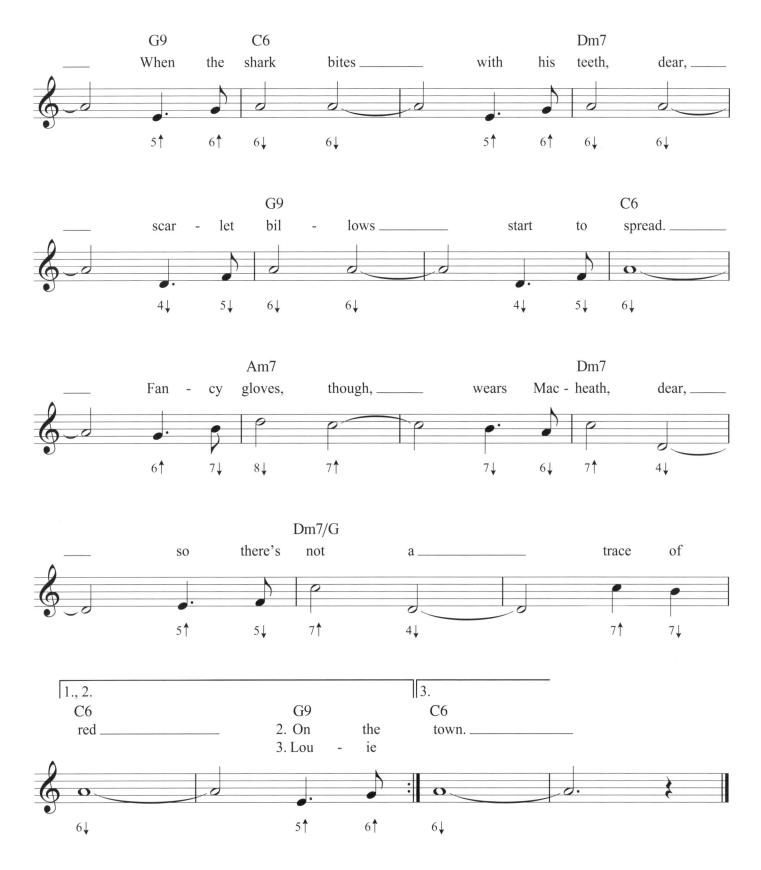

Additional Lyrics

2. On the sidewalk Sunday morning lies a body oozing life.
   Someone's sneaking 'round the corner; is the someone Mack the Knife?
   From a tugboat by the river, a cement bag's dropping down.
   The cement's just for the weight, dear; bet you Mackie's back in town.

3. Louie Miller disappeared, dear, after drawing out his cash.
   And Macheath spends like a sailor; did our boy do something rash?
   Sukey Tawdry, Jenny Diver, Polly Peachum, Luck Brown.
   Oh, the line forms on the right, dear, now that Mackie's back in town.

No Rain

Words and Music by Blind Melon

*Music sounds one octave higher than written.

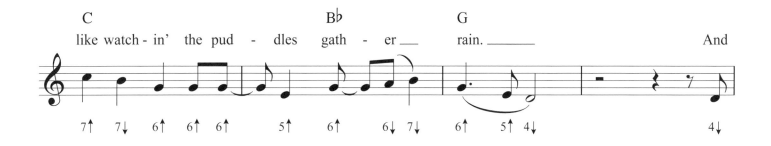

like watch-in' the pud – dles gath – er ___ rain. _____ And

7↑ 7↓ 6↑ 6↑ 6↑ 5↑ 6↑ 6↓ 7↓ 6↑ 5↑ 4↓ 4↓

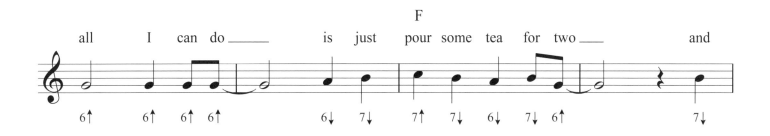

all I can do _____ is just pour some tea for two ___ and

6↑ 6↑ 6↑ 6↑ 6↓ 7↓ 7↑ 7↓ 6↓ 7↓ 6↑ 7↓

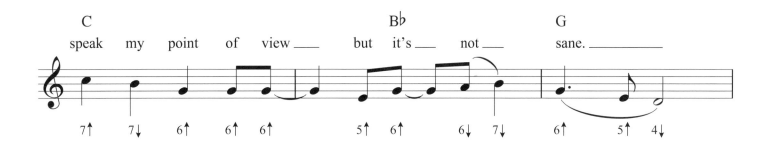

speak my point of view ___ but it's ___ not ___ sane. _____ And

7↑ 7↓ 6↑ 6↑ 6↑ 5↑ 6↑ 6↓ 7↓ 6↑ 5↑ 4↓

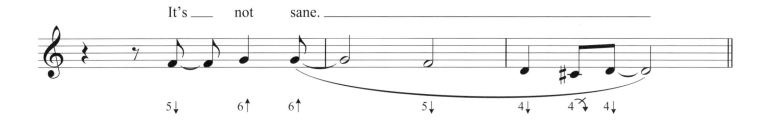

It's ___ not sane. _____

5↓ 6↑ 6↑ 5↓ 4↓ 4⤨ 4↓

𝄋 **Chorus**

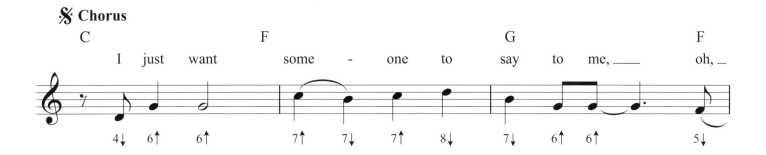

I just want some – one to say to me, ___ oh, __

4↓ 6↑ 6↑ 7↑ 7↓ 7↑ 8↓ 7↓ 6↑ 6↑ 5↓

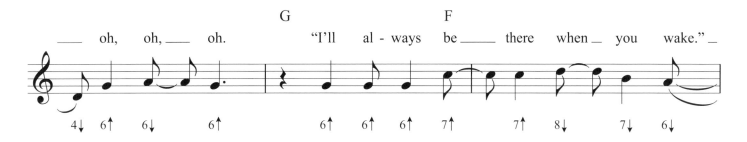

___ oh, oh, ___ oh. "I'll al – ways be ___ there when __ you wake." ___

4↓ 6↑ 6↓ 6↑ 6↑ 6↑ 6↑ 7↑ 7↑ 8↓ 7↓ 6↓

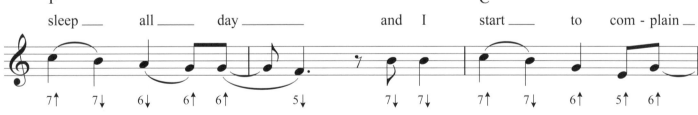

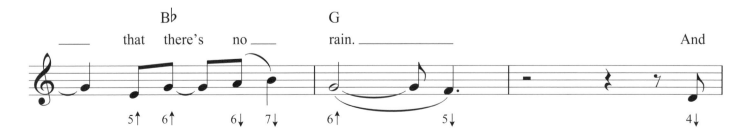

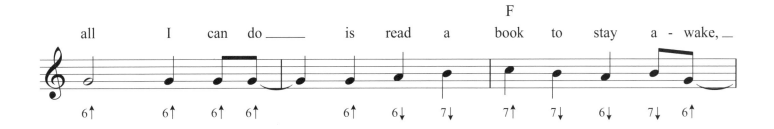

all   I   can   do ____   is   read   a   book   to   stay   a - wake, ____

F

6↑   6↑   6↑   6↑   6↑   6↓   7↓   7↑   7↓   6↓   7↓   6↑

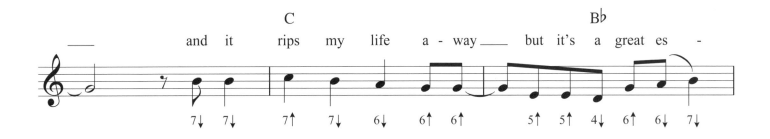

____   and   it   rips   my   life   a - way ____   but   it's   a   great   es -

C   B♭

7↓   7↓   7↑   7↓   6↓   6↑   6↑   5↑   5↑   4↓   6↑   6↓   7↓

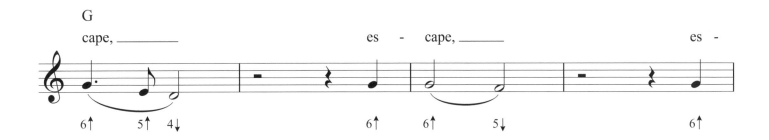

cape, _____   es - cape, _____   es -

G

6↑   5↑   4↓   6↑   6↑   5↓   6↑

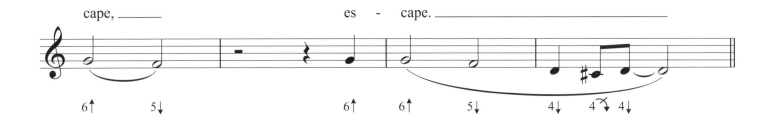

cape, ____   es - cape. _____

6↑   5↓   6↑   6↑   5↓   4↓   4↗   4↓

Verse

G

3. All   I   can   say ____   is   that   my   life   is   pret - ty   plain, ____

F

6↑   6↑   6↑   6↑   6↑   6↑   6↑   5↓   5↓   5↓   6↑   5↓

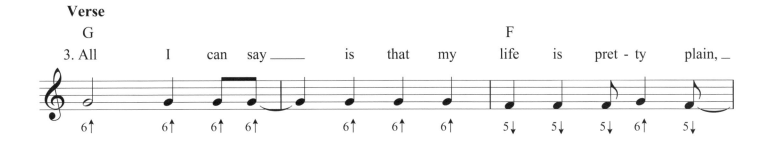

____   you   don't   like   my   point   of   view, ____   you   think   that   I'm   in -

C   B♭

5↓   5↓   5↑   5↑   5↑   4↓   5↑   4↓   6↑   4↓   5↓   6↑   6↓

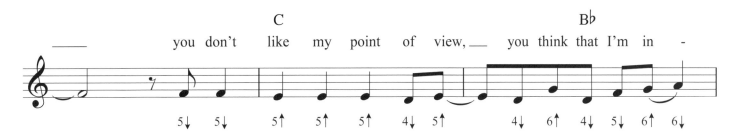

G

sane.

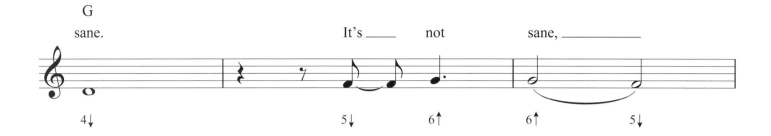

4↓

It's ___ not sane, ___

5↓ 6↑ 6↑ 5↓

D.S. al Coda

it's ___ not sane. _____

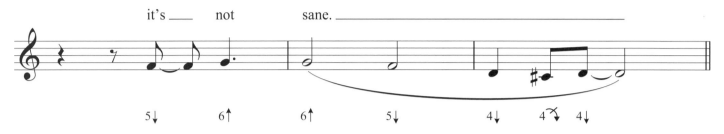

5↓ 6↑ 6↑ 5↓ 4↓ 4↷ 4↓

⊕ **Coda**

Outro

___ and I'll have it made. ___

G   F

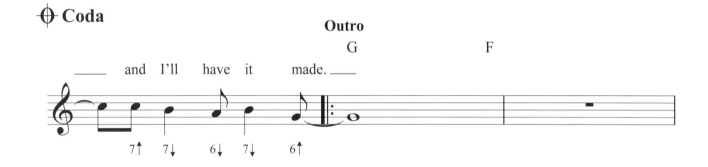

7↑ 7↓ 6↓ 7↓ 6↑

G   F

G   F

Play 3 times   *Vocal ad lib.*

G   F

Oh. _____

Oh. _____

6↑ 5↓ 5↑ 4↓

6↑ 5↓ 5↑ 4↓

G   F   N.C.

___

Oh. _____

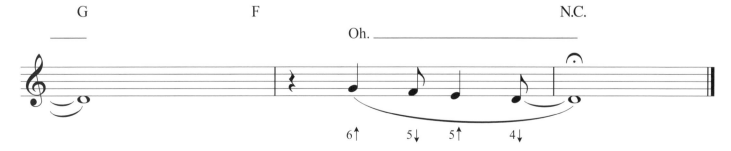

6↑ 5↓ 5↑ 4↓

Save the Last Dance for Me

Words and Music by Doc Pomus and Mort Shuman

%. **Verse**

Moderately

C

1. You can dance ev - 'ry dance with the guy who gives __
2., 3. *See additional lyrics*

4↑ 4↓ 5↑ 4↓ 5↑ 5↑ 5↑ 5↑ 5↑ 5↑ 5↑

G7

__ you the eye; let him hold you tight. __ You can

5↑ 5↑ 5↑ 5↑ 5↑ 5↑ 4↓ 4↓ 4↓ 5↑

smile __ ev - 'ry smile for the man who held __ your hand __ 'neath the

5↑ 4↓ 5↓ 5↓ 5↓ 5↓ 5↓ 5↓ 5↓ 5↓ 5↓ 6↑ 6↑ 5↓

C

pale moon - light. __ { 1., 2. But } don't for -
                    { 3. 'Cause }

5↓ 5↑ 5↑ 5↑ 5↓ 6↑

Chorus

F   C

get who's tak - ing you home __ and in whose arms you're gon - na be.

6↓ 6↓ 6↓ 6↓ 7↓ 7↑ 7↑ 8↑ 7↑ 7↓ 6↓ 6↓ 6↑ 6↑

Additional Lyrics

2. Oh, I know the music's fine
   Like sparkling wine; go and have your fun.
   Laugh and sing, but while we're apart
   Don't give your heart to anyone.

3. You can dance, go and carry on
   Till the night is gone and it's time to go.
   If he asks if you're all alone,
   Can he take you home, you must tell him no.

Nobody Does It Better

from THE SPY WHO LOVED ME

Music by Marvin Hamlisch
Lyrics by Carole Bayer Sager

*Music sounds one octave higher than written.

79

She Drives Me Crazy

Words and Music by David Steele and Roland Gift

Won't you ev - er set me free? _____ This wait - ing 'round's
What I had for you was true. _____ Things go wrong, they

Chorus

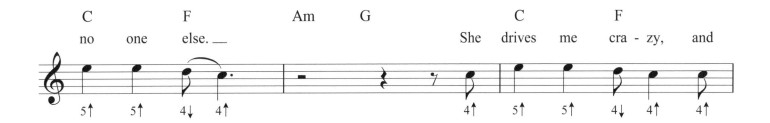

kill - ing me. ___ } She drives me cra - zy like
al - ways do. ___ }

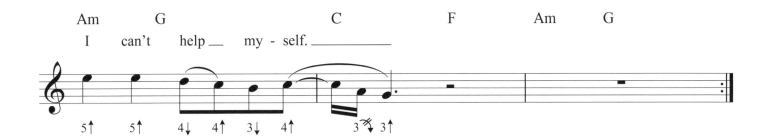

no one else. ___ She drives me cra - zy, and

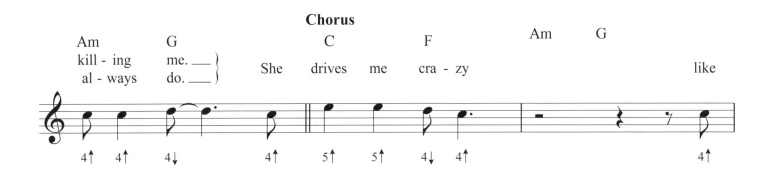

I can't help ___ my - self. _____

Interlude

Play 4 times

Verse

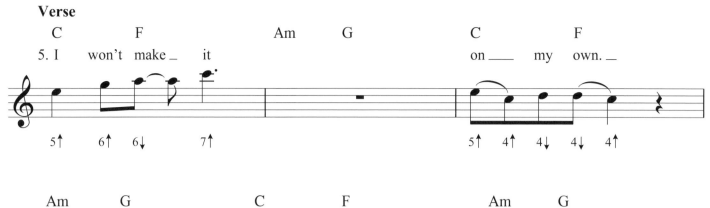

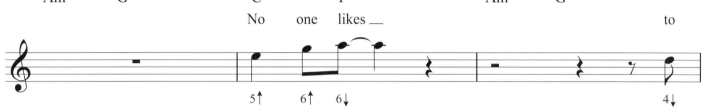

Outro-Chorus

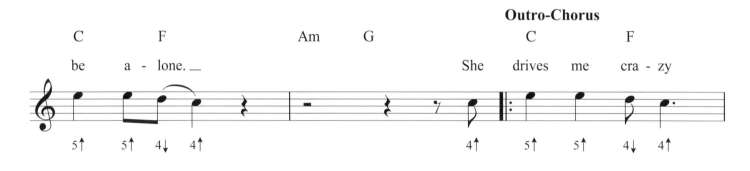

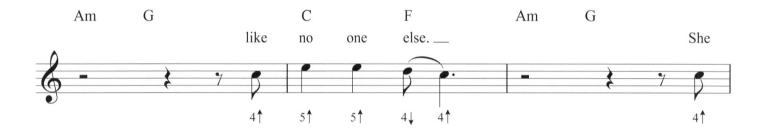

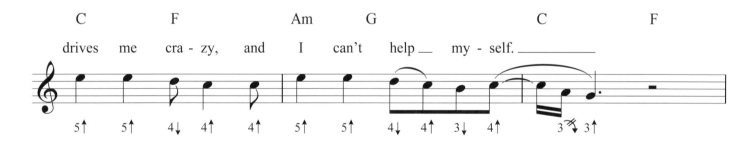

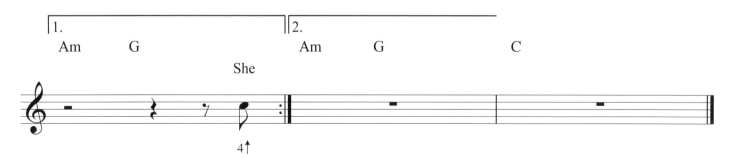

Waiting on the World to Change

Words and Music by John Mayer

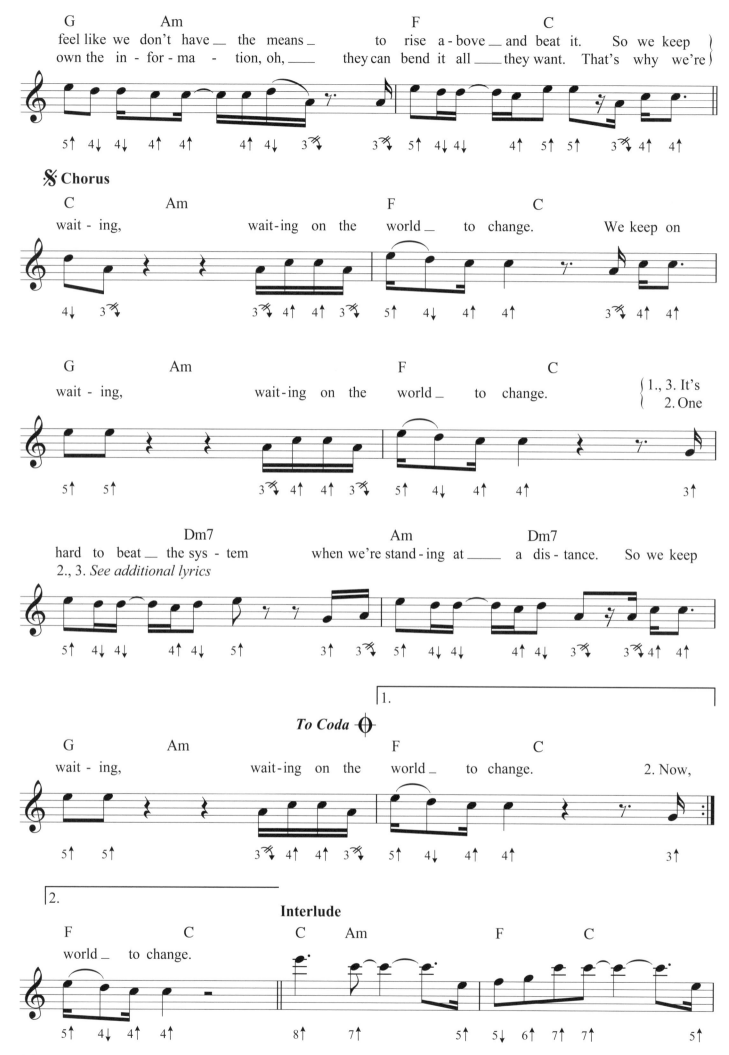

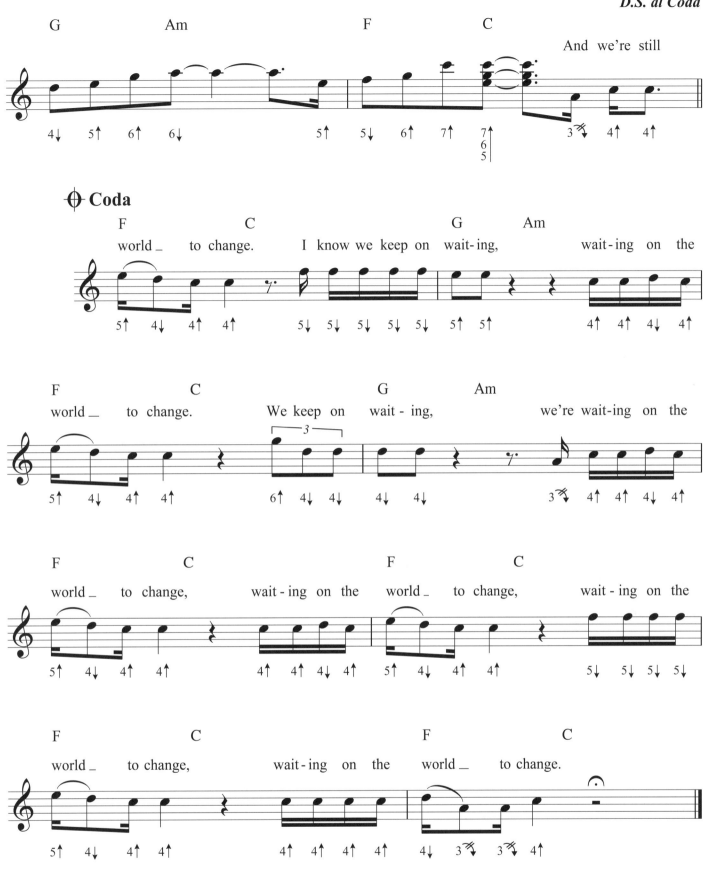

Coda

Additional Lyrics

Chorus 2. One day our generation is gonna rule the population.
So we keep on waiting, waiting on the world to change.

3. It's not that we don't care; we just know that the fight ain't fair.
So we keep on waiting, waiting on the world to change.

You've Got a Friend

Words and Music by Carole King

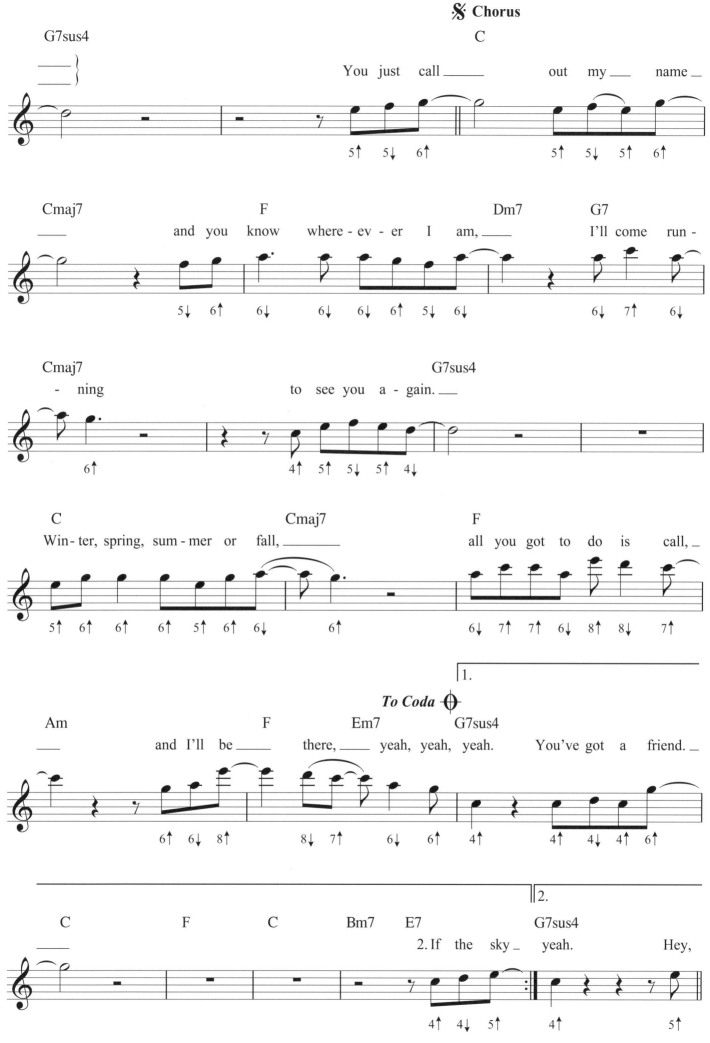

Bridge

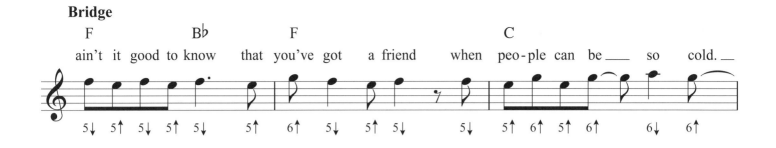

F   B♭   F   C

ain't it good to know that you've got a friend when peo-ple can be ___ so cold. ___

5↓ 5↑ 5↓ 5↑ 5↓   5↑ 6↑ 5↓ 5↑ 5↓   5↓ 5↑ 6↑ 5↑ 6↑   6↓ 6↑

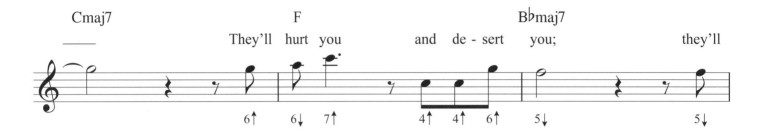

Cmaj7   F   B♭maj7

___ They'll hurt you and de - sert you; they'll

6↑ 6↓ 7↑   4↑ 4↑ 6↑ 5↓   5↓

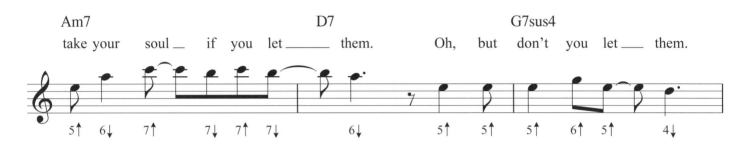

Am7   D7   G7sus4

take your soul ___ if you let ___ them. Oh, but don't you let ___ them.

5↑ 6↓ 7↑ 7↓ 7↑ 7↓   6↓   5↑ 5↑ 5↑ 6↑ 5↑ 4↓

D.S. al Coda   ⊕ **Coda**

G   G7sus4

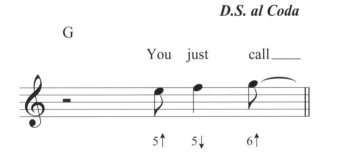 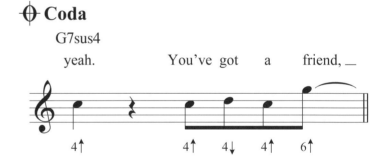

You just call ___   yeah. You've got a friend, ___

5↑ 5↓ 6↑   4↑   4↑ 4↓ 4↑ 6↑

Outro

C   F   C

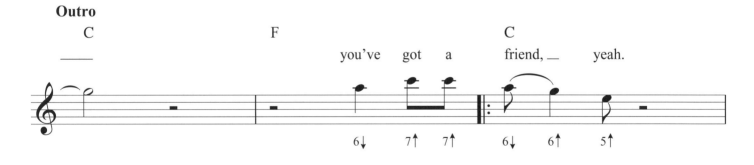

___ you've got a friend, ___ yeah.

6↓ 7↑ 7↑   6↓ 6↑ 5↑

1.
F

Ain't it good ___ to know you've got a

6↑ 6↑ 6↓ 7↑ 7↑ 6↓ 6↑ 5↑

2.
F   C

You've got a friend. ___

4↑ 4↓ 4↑ 6↑

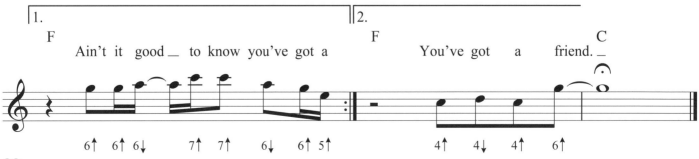